ALTERNATOR
BOOKS™

THE UNOFFICIAL GUIDE TO MINECRAFT MODS

LINDA ZAJAC

Lerner Publications ◆ Minneapolis

IN MEMORY OF DAN, A JAVA PROGRAMMER
WHO PLAYS *MINECRAFT* WITH THE STARS

Copyright © 2019 by Lerner Publishing Group, Inc.

Lerner Publications Company
A division of Lerner Publishing Group, Inc.
241 First Avenue North
Minneapolis, MN 55401 USA

For reading levels and more information, look up this title at www.lernerbooks.com.

Main body text set in Aptifer Slab LT Pro 11.5/18.
Typeface provided by Linotype AG.

Library of Congress Cataloging-in-Publication Data

Names: Zajac, Linda, 1960– author.
Title: The unofficial guide to Minecraft mods / Linda Zajac.
Description: Minneapolis : Lerner Publications, 2019. | Series: My Minecraft
   (Alternator Books) | Includes bibliographical references and index. | Audience:
   Age 7–11. | Audience: Grade 4 to 6.
Identifiers: LCCN 2018022641 (print) | LCCN 2018023487 (ebook) | ISBN 9781541543539
   (eb pdf) | ISBN 9781541538863 (lb : alk. paper) | ISBN 9781541546127 (pb : alk. paper)
Subjects: LCSH: Minecraft (Game)—Juvenile literature.
Classification: LCC GV1469.35.M535 (ebook) | LCC GV1469.35.M535 Z35 2019 (print) |
   DDC 794.8—dc23

LC record available at https://lccn.loc.gov/2018022641

Manufactured in the United States of America
1-45069-35896-8/9/2018

CONTENTS

PIG TROUBLE

AS MORNING SUNSHINE SPILLS ACROSS THE *MINECRAFT* WORLD, YOU CLIMB ABOARD A WOODEN BOAT. Every stroke of the oars takes you closer to an island. While you're exploring the island, a pig plops down inside your boat. The pig has to go before you can sail again, but it refuses to budge. What are you going to do?

A rowboat is easy to build, but *Minecraft* has lots of other ways to get around too.

In *Minecraft*, a stubborn pig doesn't have to put a dent in your travel plans. By using mods, you have lots of transportation options. *Mods* is short for "modifications." Mods are code, or instructions that computers can follow, that can change nearly every part of the game. With mods, you can soar in a rocket ship, ride an ostrich, or even fly with a dragon. *Yee-haw!*

CHAPTER 1
A MISHMASH OF MODS

MINECRAFT IS AN ADVENTURE IN MINING, EXPLORING, AND BUILDING.
Minecraft's creator, Markus "Notch" Persson, released the game in 2009. Millions of people play it every day. One of the reasons it's so popular is that mods allow you to change the game. *Minecraft* gamers have made thousands of mods.

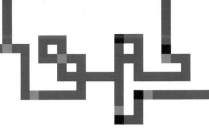

Mods can make it easier to explore *Minecraft*'s vast world.

With mods, you can make *Minecraft* the way you want it to be. You can add building materials to your **inventory**, or explore without getting lost. While camping in a cave, you might decide you'd rather live in a city. If you're journeying among jungle trees or jagged mountain peaks, you might welcome a map. Or maybe your character hungers for a cheeseburger and fries.

Some mods let you instantly make machines such as vehicles or even entire buildings. Mods add sounds to the game such as crickets chirping or owls hooting. They can make hostile **mobs** such as dragons and big cats appear. Some mods are just plain silly. They might allow you to create crazy hats and rubber chickens. You can even add rainbow cats that fart.

Vehicles such as trikes and bumper cars make getting around fun.

Rainbow cats add a splash of color to *Minecraft*.

Modders write new code or add to existing code to make mods. Like *Minecraft*, mods are written in **Java**, a programming language. Modders use their coding skills to turn their ideas into reality.

Writing new *Minecraft* code can take a lot of time. Many modders share their creations online. Their reward is the thrill of knowing others are playing the game with mods they designed.

STEMCRAFT

Some code has mistakes called **bugs**. It's easy to make mistakes while coding, and early versions of *Minecraft* had a lot of bugs. When Persson tried to create a pig for the game, he mixed up the code for height and length. Persson thought the upright creature was creepy, so he named it creeper and kept it in the game. Creepers sneak up on your character. When they get close enough, they explode.

Minecraft is so popular that it made Markus Persson one of the richest people in the world.

Mods such as Pam's HarvestCraft, which adds new food to *Minecraft*, have been tested by thousands of gamers.

Modders share their work by posting mods on *Minecraft* community websites. Some gamers package several mods together in a bundle called a **mod pack**. With thousands of options to choose from, looking for a new mod is like being in a candy store. To find the best mods, look for mods that have been **downloaded** many times. Popular mods are less likely to have bugs— players wouldn't keep downloading them if they had problems. If a mod has coding errors, it could ruin your *Minecraft* worlds.

To avoid downloading mods that will ruin your game or computer, download mods only from trustworthy sites such as Planet Minecraft and CurseForge. And be sure to ask an adult before downloading anything from the internet. Mods are easy to add to your game. Work slowly and carefully, and you'll be less likely to make a mistake.

A bug can ruin your *Minecraft* construction project, destroy your *Minecraft* world, or even harm your computer.

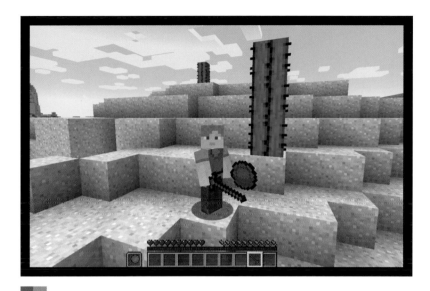

This character is holding a sword called a rapier and a frying pan that a gamer added to *Minecraft* with a mod.

Before adding mods to your game, **back up** your *Minecraft* files. That way you have copies of all the worlds you created in case a mod with an error ruins them. Look online for instructions about backing up your *Minecraft* worlds.

With your *Minecraft* files copied, you're almost ready to look for mods. But before downloading anything, you need a way to load them into your game. You need Forge.

CHAPTER 2

FORGE ONWARD

FORGE IS A PROGRAM THAT LETS YOU ADD MODS TO *MINECRAFT.* It's one of the easiest and most popular methods of adding mods to the game. Before starting a new *Minecraft* world, Forge searches your computer for the mods you've downloaded. It lets you play with or without mods.

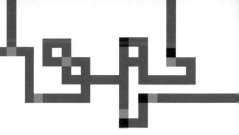

Mojang, the company behind *Minecraft*, often releases updated versions of the game. The versions might add new building materials, tools, or mobs. They might correct bugs from previous versions.

Every time Mojang releases a *Minecraft* update, modders test their mods to make sure they work with the new version of the game. If not, they adjust the code and test their mods again until they work. This takes time, so the mod you want may not be up to date right after a new version of the game comes out.

The Forge home screen has options to help you manage your mods.

CODECRAFT

Markus Persson created *Minecraft* in Java, an **object-oriented programming language**. Java programmers use combinations of symbols and words to create computer code. Java code describes each object by the way it looks. An object in *Minecraft* might be a block of dirt, an apple, or a creeper.

Objects are defined by their properties such as color, texture, or hardness. The code can also describe how and when an object moves and how fast it goes.

Objects aren't always solid things. In *Minecraft*, fire, weather, and explosions are objects. Java code describes how they look, how they move, and how they interact with other objects. For example, fire will spread to an object made of wood, but not to a metal object.

Fire can spread quickly, so be careful where you place it.

The *Minecraft* home screen shows the game's version number and other information.

Before downloading Forge, make sure to select the right version. The version of Forge and the mods that you download must match the *Minecraft* version on your computer. To find your *Minecraft* version, start the game. The version number appears on the bottom of the screen.

CHAPTER 3
WELCOME TO MODMART

GAMERS FROM ALL OVER THE WORLD HAVE SPENT COUNTLESS HOURS CREATING A HUGE LIBRARY OF MODS. With thousands of mods to choose from, the choices can be overwhelming. Thankfully, you don't have to choose just one. You can play the game with multiple mods installed at the same time.

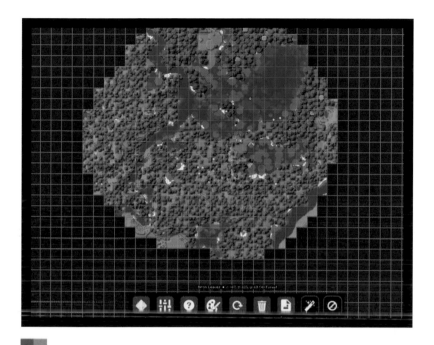

The JourneyMap mod helps you find things in *Minecraft* you may have missed.

Suppose you've fired up a new game and turned on the JourneyMap mod. As you're trekking across your world, the mod helps you navigate. Steep peaks, towering trees, or dense jungle plants might block your view. You're lost! With JourneyMap, you can see an overhead map of your surroundings. You can display it on-screen as a minimap or switch to full-screen and zoom in on the details.

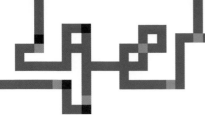

To the east on your map, you spot a red dot. The dot stands for a hostile mob. You head south instead, where a quiet river flows. As you race across the landscape, JourneyMap helps you avoid hostile mobs, lava, and other dangers.

Creepers and lava are best avoided.

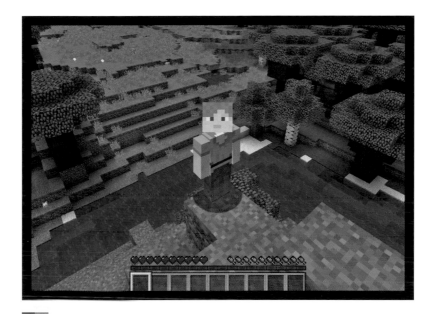

Mods can add lots of familiar sights and sounds to the *Minecraft* landscape.

The Dynamic Surroundings mod enhances your game's sound effects. The mod adds new sounds to *Minecraft* that help make the game feel more realistic. Your footsteps crunch as you walk on gravel along the river. Thunder rumbles in the distance. The sound of flowing water grows louder, and soon you hear it rushing over a waterfall. Dynamic Surroundings also adds visual effects such as bubbles in water and fireflies at night.

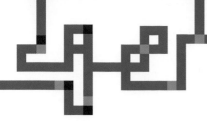

Mods such as Pam's HarvestCraft help your character heal quickly after an injury.

As you explore near the waterfall, you slip off a low ledge. You're injured! You can hear your heart pounding loudly and clearly: *thump, thump, thump.*

You need food to heal, so you scout out the open fields by the river's edge. With Pam's HarvestCraft mod loaded, you discover all kinds of new vegetables: okra, cabbages, turnips, parsnips, and rutabagas. Pam's HarvestCraft lets gamers create recipes for sushi, hot wings, pizza, and more. But you need to have the right ingredients in your inventory to make them. Since you have mostly vegetables, you make do with turnip soup and a side of okra chips. *Nom, nom.*

Feeling stronger after eating, you follow a bright blue butterfly as it flits through the forest. Crickets chirp and fireflies twinkle. You're so focused on the butterfly that you don't notice the red dots that are getting nearer on your map. Suddenly, two big black bears roar. You run for your life!

Black bears are one of four kinds of bears you can add to *Minecraft*.

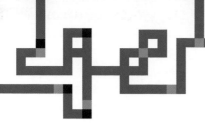

After you've tamed an elephant, you can ride it.

With the Mo' Creatures mod, you can add dozens of new mobs to your *Minecraft* experience. You'll get the ability to tame and ride some of them too. The mod adds creatures of all sizes, from elephants to maggots. It even includes fantasy beasts such as ogres, werewolves, and **wyverns**. Be careful when you explore the *Minecraft* world with Mo' Creatures!

CHAPTER 4

FLASH FORWARD

MINECRAFT MODDERS ARE CONSTANTLY CHANGING THE GAME WITH MODS. They get their ideas from movies, other video games, and things they see and do. The people behind _Minecraft_ get ideas from the real world too. Jens Bergensten, lead creative designer for _Minecraft_, noticed fancy tiles on a floor in a hotel in California. They gave him the idea to add colorful building blocks to the game.

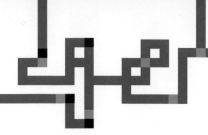

Update Aquatic opens a whole new world for modders to explore.

Mojang keeps working to improve *Minecraft*. A recent update allows gamers to play together on different platforms. That way a gamer on a computer can play with a friend using an Xbox One. Update Aquatic, released in 2018, enriches the ocean with sunken ships, splashy coral, and speedy dolphins. It also makes it easier to build beneath the sea. Modders are hard at work creating fun new ways to play with Update Aquatic.

Each year, Mojang celebrates everything about *Minecraft* with MineCon. The event includes skits, contests, interviews, and much more. You can livestream the show around the world on most internet-connected devices. The *Minecraft* community can get involved too. That's you! Enter contests to win free tickets to attend the show in person.

You can often see celebrities at MineCon, such as actor Will Arnett (*left*).

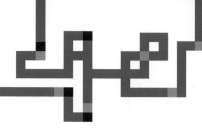

Jens Bergensten talks about the future of *Minecraft* at MineCon.

As *Minecraft* changes, so do the mods. Every new version of the game alters the experience and sparks fresh ideas from modders. By adding mods to *Minecraft*, you can reach beyond the game's limits and into the depths of your wildest imagination. What new mods will people create in the years to come?

STEMCRAFT

Long lines of computer code may look like an unfamiliar language to many people. Programmers code games and apps in different languages, including Python, Ruby, and Java. Each language has its own rules, symbols, and special words. Programmers must follow the rules carefully. If there's a bug anywhere in the code, the program might not run, or work, as expected.

It takes a lot of practice with a programming language to create a video game world.

GLOSSARY

back up: make a copy of something

bugs: errors in computer code that cause the code to work incorrectly

downloaded: transferred files or data from one computer to another

inventory: a list of resources such as building materials and tools that a character carries

Java: the programming language used to create *Minecraft*

mobs: monsters and other living things in *Minecraft*

modders: *Minecraft* fans who create and share mods

mod pack: a collection of mods

object-oriented programming language: a type of programming language based on the creation and description of objects

wyverns: creatures that look like dragons with two legs and wings

FURTHER INFORMATION

Cornell, Kari. Minecraft *Creator Markus "Notch" Persson*. Minneapolis: Lerner Publications, 2016.

Guthals, Sarah. Minecraft *Modding for Kids for Dummies*. Hoboken, NJ: John Wiley & Sons, 2015.

Learn Computer Science
https://code.org/student

LearnToMod: Code with *Minecraft*
https://www.learntomod.com

Minecraft Official Site
https://minecraft.net/en-us

Planet Minecraft: *Minecraft* Mods
https://www.planetminecraft.com/resources/mods

Schwartz, Heather E. *The World of* Minecraft. Minneapolis: Lerner Publications, 2018.

Whale, David, and Martin O'Hanlon. *Adventures in* Minecraft. Indianapolis: John Wiley and Sons, 2017.

INDEX

PHOTO ACKNOWLEDGMENTS

Image credits: Various screenshots by Linda Zajac; Mojang Official Game Developers Conference/Flickr (CC By 2.0), p. 10; Minecraft, *MINECON Earth 2017 Livestream* via YouTube, pp. 27, 28. Design element: COLCU/Shutterstock.com.